I TOOK THE
DARE

One Book. One Social Experiment.
Eighteen Young Writers.

Edited by Cynthea Liu

PIVOTAL PUBLISHING

I Took the Dare: One Book. One Social Experiment. Eighteen Young Writers.

ISBN 978-0-99903-320-3

About this Book

By Cynthea Liu

When my second children's book for young readers, *Paris Pan Takes the Dare* (Putnam, 2009), was about to be released, I wanted to do something special to introduce this book to the world. Paris Pan is more to me than just a fun novel about a twelve-year-old who takes a dare in the woods. Underneath the humor and the suspense, Paris Pan's story is also about dealing with the everyday life of a pre-teen in general—friendship issues, boy/girl problems, and even a family crisis. Many of the things that happened in the book happened to me, and one of the biggest things I struggled with throughout adolescence was being true to myself.

Peer pressure, popularity contests, and staying out of trouble were the name of the game during my youth. I didn't always dare to be me, and in Paris Pan, you can see what happens when you don't live up to your own standards—total mayhem!

As an author reliving her own childhood and writing it down, I got to fix all the ways in which I might have gone wrong in the past through my character Paris Pan. Paris finds a way to make things right in the end, and I guess one could also say that writing the book was therapy for me, too.

And that was how the "Take the Dare: Dare to be You" essay contest was born. What if I could catch kids in the act now and make them write about it? I asked students to think of a situation where they weren't being true to themselves, dare themselves to change for at least a week, then write an essay. The results from that social experiment are now forever memorialized in this book. I hope you enjoy their stories as much as I do.

Every time I re-read these essays, I hear the voices of the authors loud and clear. This contest may have changed some of the authors for the better, but it's also changed me. I will never forget these kids and what they had to say about their lives. I also know I will want to keep hearing more stories from more voices as the years go by. If you know of a student or class who might love to participate in the next edition of *I Took the Dare,* visit cynthealiu.com and let me know!

CONTENTS

Preface
By Cynthea Liu, Editor

As a kid, I never took writing very seriously as a career. When I was really young, I thought I was going to be a movie star like Shirley Temple and sing and dance for the big screen. Then I realized I couldn't sing *or* dance, and sadly, my Hollywood dreams were shattered. Eventually, I changed career goals (to my parents' relief)! I had always loved biology; perhaps I would be a doctor and make lots of money.

I went on to college with pre-med aspirations. But after a couple of semesters of doctor-type courses, I had to face facts—patients would be better off with physicians who understood organic chemistry. So I decided to be an Economics major. Supply and demand? Now *that* I could handle. Plus, I figured a degree related to business would make me some decent bucks, too. Notice a theme here?

Post-college, after some time in the corporate world, I realized that the money was great, but something wasn't right. I longed do something more *creative*. After I'd had enough of spreadsheets, pie charts, and long commutes, I finally quit. To my own disbelief, I took up fiction writing as a profession. Yes, writing. Me? Really?

The strange thing about my journey so far is that all along, from elementary school through college, I was often told I was a great writer, and I never believed them. I assumed the grown-ups were just doing their jobs—make the kid feel good about herself! So I kept plugging along with different career goals, hoping I'd find my real match. I might have even avoided the very things my teachers said I should pursue, just to prove them wrong.

Looking back, I totally get it now. My teachers weren't trying to make me feel better about myself. They were trying to make me *see myself.* Today, I am happy to say, I have never loved anything more than being a writer. Yes, I L-O-V-E what I do, and that is priceless.

To the essayists, congratulations! I hope you will continue to share your writing talents with others, no matter if you have dreams of becoming doctors or dancers, movie-makers or botanists, or just plain-don't-know-what-you're-going-to-do. And I'm *not* just saying that to make you feel good. Your words mean something. It's not just writing. It's an expression of *you.*

I dare you to keep being you. That's something priceless, too.

In fact, I triple-dog-dare you.

Cynthea Liu spent most of her formative years in Oklahoma and Texas, where she was a member of the Whiz Quiz team, an academic decathloner, and a spelling bee champion. (Yes, she was very popular.) After attending college on the East Coast, she landed a job as a management consultant.

When she had enough of PowerPoint and frequent flyer miles, she traded in her suit for sweats to focus on the fun stuff—writing for children. Read more about Cynthea at **www.cynthealiu.com**

Emily took the DARE

The Challenge of a Friend
By Emily Cho, Grade 2

I had a dreadful classmate at my school. The first time I saw her, I instantly knew that she was not going to be my friend. She was very sensitive, which I didn't like. If I touched a part of the table that was near her, she got mad at me because she thought that was very bothersome. She really didn't like me. As a matter of fact, I didn't like her either; she was my enemy! We tried to get each other into trouble. For example, if we fought, we went to the teacher and blamed the other person. When we got angry at each other, we said hurtful things to each other.

Days passed, and things didn't change. Actually, she annoyed me more. Although I didn't like her, sometimes I felt bad after I said hurtful things to her. Other times I felt bad for her because no one would play with her at recess or talk with her at lunch.

One day, I read about the Take the Dare competition and decided to dare myself to make friends with my enemy. I dared myself to show her that I am not a mean person, but a kind person.

On the first day, I tried to be nice, but failed. I asked her if I could look at the picture in her panda article, but she said no and got mad at me. I knew that it would not be easy, but I was still determined to make friends with her.

On the second day, it didn't go well either. In research time, and many other times, I tried to be nice to her. I tried to talk to her whenever I had a chance, but she would just get annoyed. I felt annoyed too because she would not listen to what I had to say if I didn't treat her very nicely. She still didn't like me. *No wonder.* I was trying, but I had to admit that I still didn't like her either. Still, I was determined to be patient and go on.

On the third day, we had so much snow. At recess, I saw her playing with a big group of kids on the playground. I decided to go and ask her if she wanted to play with me. To my surprise, she said yes. She wanted to make a slide out of snow. To me, it sounded like the most boring project to do on the day when we had so much snow! Anyway, I decided to play with her for a while. As expected, it wasn't fun for me, so I played with someone else. When I left her playing by the slide herself, I felt a little sorry for her. I felt guilty because it seemed like I was not very dedicated to my dare project, but that was not true.

On the fourth day, nothing happened. I didn't have a chance to eat or play with her. I hoped the last day would be the best day. And it happened. I finally got to play with her and I thought she was pretty nice to me. I felt very good because I think she got to know that I was a kind person. On the first day, it was very hard to be nice. As a few days passed, I knew what she liked me doing with her and saying to her, and things that she didn't like.

Looking back, making friends has not been easy. In fact, it was very hard. Even though her words had been hurtful to me, I had to be patient and understanding. I am glad that I didn't give up on my dare.

Through this dare project, I experienced two things. First, I got to participate in a wonderful competition. Second, I changed one of my worst enemies into a good friend.

Emily enjoys reading, writing, and drawing. She wants to be an animal activist when she grows up.

Isabella took the
DARE

The Waking Up Early and Making Breakfast Challenge
By Isabella Cho, Grade 2

I love to sleep and I have a hard time waking up early. Sometimes, I can't even hear my alarm clock. Even if I hear it, I just pretend to sleep until my parents come and say I only have 20 minutes left before we need to leave for school. When I go downstairs, I feel exhausted and not very cheerful. At times, I am so late that I can't eat breakfast, and then I am hungry at school! Plus, when I eat, it makes me late for school. I wondered if there was any way things could change.

One day, I heard about the Take the Dare competition. I desperately wanted to participate since I knew if I did I hopefully would get better at waking up. I was so excited that I set two goals of not only waking up early, but also helping my mom make breakfast. I set these two goals because I thought they would be great habits and would also be tremendously helpful to my parents.

On the first day, I felt very tired when my parents woke me up. I used to wake up at 7:30 a.m., but it was 7:15 a.m.!

I was still a little grumpy about having to wake up early, but I knew I would feel better. I managed to dress myself and went downstairs. I told my mom I was ready. My mom said that today I would make toast. I said "okay" because I knew that making toast would be an easy job for me to do. When I was done taking the bread out of the freezer, toasting it, and putting jam on it, I even cut the burnt parts off, which my mom didn't even ask me to do! I felt like I had accomplished my first task.

On the second morning, I felt very frustrated because my parents made me wake up early again. I remembered asking my parents to wake me up early and I regretted it. When I went downstairs, I gradually became cheerful. I made cereal for breakfast. I even cleaned a mess my mom made.

On the third morning, I felt happy crawling out of my covers. When I went downstairs, my mom told me to peel sweet potatoes. It was not easy, but I felt proud of myself for doing all the hard work.

On the fourth morning, I got dressed as quick as lightning and went downstairs to see that nobody was there. That day, I felt like I had really accomplished my dare goal. I guessed that my mom was taking a shower. I enjoyed a quick bowl of cereal by myself. I felt very peaceful. I also felt very happy. When I saw my sisters hurrying downstairs, I smiled to myself, thinking, *if only they had woken up as early as me!*

On the last morning, since there was no school, I woke up at 8 a.m., but I was still able to help my mom make breakfast. When I went downstairs, my mom was just about to start making breakfast. My mom said since there was no school, we could have a special dish of Korean rice and egg. "Yes!" I said. That was my favorite breakfast treat. Cracking eggs, adding all different kinds of sauces, and putting it in the microwave was hard, but it was also very fun! I had a smile on my face when I saw the last "Take the Dare" breakfast. We all agreed that it was the best out of all five mornings!

This dare helped me get into the habit of waking up early and helping out. At first, I felt exhausted, but as I got the hang of it, I felt more excited. Now I think it is a great habit! I learned that waking up early really helps my parents. My mom is also very proud of me because I helped out. It made a big change.

Isabella is an enthusiastic reader and avid artist. She hopes to be a botanist when she grows up.

Brady took the DARE

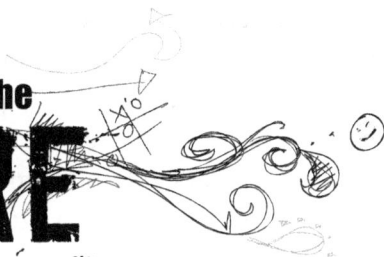

I am a Cheetah Now!
By Brady James Brazda, Grade 3

"Be a cheetah, not a turtle," Mom tells me every morning. I do not like waking up in the morning, and I am slow like a turtle. I love school. It is just that it is hard for me to wake up and move fast in the morning. I move quickly on the tennis court during team practices and during lacrosse and basketball. But every morning, it seems hard to move fast and get ready, even though I really am not a slow kid.

I read in the morning instead of moving fast. My mom bought me an awesome bunk bed. She also bought me a cool blue light that clips on to my bed under the top bunk so that I can read any time I want. I love to read! I read nonfiction books so I can learn lots of stuff. My favorite book is *Deadliest Catch*. It is about the show on Discovery Channel. Crabbers catch crab in the Bering Sea and have lots of adventures. I figure this is why my mom does not get too mad at me—she likes it when I read.

My mom is a teacher. She knows I love to write stories and illustrate them. Sometimes I do that in the morning, too. I take my stories and pictures to my teacher at school for her to see and read.

My sister Halle always tells me I am slow, too. She is in sixth grade this year. She just started going to a new middle school. Halle tells me that when I move slowly, it stresses her and Mommy out because they could be late for both schools. My mom and Halle read about the Take the Dare contest and dared me to "move like a cheetah, not like a turtle" for a week. A few weeks ago, Halle set her cell phone next to my bunk bed because it has a cool loud ringer. It went off every morning and I jumped out of bed, got dressed really fast, ate the granola bars I eat for breakfast, brushed my teeth, and got my backpack ready. I walked into my mom's room on the first day of the dare and she was still doing her hair. I told her I was all ready for school and moved like a cheetah! She could not believe it!

Then I went to Halle's room, and she was still getting ready for school, and she could not believe that I was ready before her! I thought it was great because I moved so quickly and no one had to tell me to move that way. I also love my mom and sister so much, so I was happy that I made them so happy and did not stress them out.

For the rest of the week, I did just what I did in that first day. I learned a lot from doing the dare. By moving faster, I even had time to build with my Legos before school. Oh, I love Legos, too! My mom even surprised me with a small Lego set for doing such a great job during the week, so even if I do not win this contest, I got something special from her. I am proud of myself for moving like a cheetah, and I know my mom and sister are proud of me, too. I will move like a cheetah every morning!

Brady is an honor roll student and lives in Houston. His hobbies include writing, art, and building with Legos. He is an exceptional athlete.

Shirowid took the DARE

Take a Stand! Be Yourself!

By Shirowid Sharma, Grade 3

I always think about why it took so long for me to understand my situation. I am a third grader. I am a grown-up kid. Also, my teacher says I am very social and intelligent, too. So why do I keep forgetting important things?

We came to this city just four months back, and I started attending this new school. Initially everything was fine, and I was doing well in the class. After a month or so, I felt like not being attentive and didn't perform much in the class. Every other day, I was earning a "News Flash" from school for homework that wasn't done or for not paying attention. At first, I tried to resolve the problems, but I couldn't. Slowly it became more complicated. I wasn't feeling happy in school. Sometimes, I forgot to bring back my lunch box or, most often, to stack my chair at the end of the day. The more I tried to remember everything in school, the more I kept forgetting. I started wondering why I had to go to school every day. Was it necessary? Maybe I was feeling bad because I wasn't getting attention in class like I once had.

One day, my teacher said, "I want to see your mom."

I was surprised. "Why?" I asked. Did I do something wrong? I had never hurt anybody. What could be the reason? Wasn't the News Flash enough to tell my mother that I was having trouble?

Finally, Mom went to the school and met my classroom teacher. They had a long discussion in private. After some time, my teacher called me in and said, "Son, I know from the last few weeks, you haven't been yourself. You forget many things in class. Also, most of the time, I feel as if you aren't paying attention. This does not reflect who you truly are. Your mom and I would like to help you. But before we do, you need to make a promise. From now on, you have to dare to be yourself, like you were before!"

That was the moment that made me think about how much they really care for me.

"First," my teacher continued, "make a list of the important work you have to do almost *every day*. It could be your homework or a play date with your friend.

Make a chart or mark a calendar at home. You can ask your mom to print you a month-long calendar. You could mark it for important dates and work. Second, do not forget to look at the calendar the very first thing in the morning every day. Try this for the next two weeks; you'll see a change in yourself for sure."

My mom added, "You can also use a Post-It to write a to-do list, and then stick it someplace where you can see it easily."

I liked the idea and promised to do so, for I knew that I was a good kid.

My mission to change myself began that very same day. I made a list of all those things that were very important in school and at home. Then I marked my calendar accordingly. I marked Monday for "return library books," Tuesday for "wear sneakers for P.E.," and so on. I also marked every day from Monday to Friday to remind myself about my daily routine responsibilities. I also wrote on a Post-It with items such as "stack my chair," "bring lunch box," and "bring daily homework folder" and stuck it to my desk to remind myself about them.

A few days later, I felt confident. It had been a week, and I hadn't had any News Flashes. I always finished my homework and turned it in on time. I also scored well on science tests. In short, neither my mom nor my teacher had any complaints about me.

My message to all kids like me is that at any point in time, if you ever feel like not being yourself, you should definitely take the dare to make a change. Try not to forget about important things. When you act smart and wise, you are an example to others about how one can overcome any difficult situation. Don't forget! Take a stand! Be yourself!

Shirowid started writing at seven. He wants to be an astronaut and he loves to play games and watch SpongeBob Squarepants. *His favorite color is orange.*

Abigail took the DARE

One Week of Change
By Abigail Lindner, Grade 4

This week was really difficult. I dared myself to be me. I act shy when I communicate with people. I don't look them in the eye. I pull at my clothes and speak quietly. These actions tell others that I'm shy. I have a great imagination, but whenever I come up with a fun idea, I never share it. The thing is, I'm not timid at all! I'm actually a really funny person.

Throughout the week, I had many opportunities to try my dare. In the beginning of my dare week, I went to the park to meet one of my mom's friends. I made sure to make eye contact and speak strongly. It was a little hard at first, but when I continued for a while, I became comfortable. Over the weekend at church, I led the music on stage by doing the hand motions to the songs. I usually go all noodle-like, but instead I stood up as straight as a stick and didn't pull at my clothes. Then, during the week at school, I had a meeting with my class newspaper friends. We were having trouble choosing a survey question. I had an idea about green vegetables, since it was the March edition and spring had sprung. Instead of keeping it to myself, I shared it. I felt great when it was out. Everyone even liked my idea! Each school day, when I was crossing the street on my way to school, I looked the crossing guard in the eye when she spoke to me, something I don't usually do.

When the week started, I thought it was impossible to accomplish my dare. The very thought of looking someone in the eye made me feel awkward inside. I felt like I had a million tiny people dancing in my stomach. As the week progressed, I began to have more confidence that I was going to finish my dare. Little by little, the doubt and nervousness disappeared. By the end of week, I was making eye contact, standing straighter, and leaving my clothes alone. In the end, I learned how to show others that I am a confident, funny person. I'm glad I took the dare because it helped me to illustrate what kind of person I am and not what I appeared to be.

Abigail has loved writing stories as long as she can remember. When she isn't writing, she enjoys reading, crafting, and spending time with her family.

Grace took the DARE

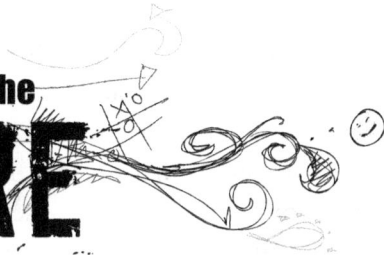

I Dared to Desert Dessert
By Grace Patton, Grade 5

It all started when an author came to visit my school. Sitting among my friends, chattering away, our yakking jerked to a stop as soon as the author walked on to the temporary stage. She talked about everything, or at least everything every author says in front of a school group: childhood, life right now, and inspiration for her book. Out of that script, there was a line that I had never heard an author speak before: "I really don't like writing, but I do it for the outcome. Not for the money. I do it for the fans' pleasure."

The author continued talking, and after the speech, she dared us to write an essay. Not just any essay, but a *dare* essay. I went home and got right to work. As

I sat, considering the dare, I recognized a connection between the dare and the upcoming church season! I decided to dare myself to not eat dessert. But not for just one week—*the entire Lenten period.* After all, Jesus had to give up a lot more than chocolate milk!

The moments when I almost gave up were always either in the cafeteria or at The Cheesecake Factory. There were several things that I noticed during my period of torture. One, the school cafeteria always serves the best desserts during Lent. Maybe they are trying to test our resolve? They served chocolate cake, cinnamon buns, cinnamon bars, and many more scrumptious desserts. Two, The Cheesecake Factory serves my favorite dessert of all time—Godiva Chocolate Cheesecake. Three, through all my suffering, I was able to find a couple of loopholes. If you look carefully, you will see the there are forty-four days between Lent and Easter. The Lenten period is only *forty* days; it does not include Sundays! Therefore, you can feast with dessert every Sunday. Also, I figured something sweet was only a dessert if eaten immediately following a meal. Otherwise, the sweet was just a snack!

As it turns out, I ate a lot more sweets during the dare than I had before "giving up" dessert. With the dare, I always ate dessert on Sundays. During the dare, all I could think about was eating something sweet, so I ate a lot of snacks.

In the end, though, I failed. I gave up. I could not go without dessert for more than two weeks. My mom did not like the dare and was even trying to make me give up. She said, "You're eating more sweets than I have ever seen you eat. So give up and have dessert!" I think the moment I truly cracked was when they served cinnamon bars in the cafeteria. But I'm glad I made the dare because I learned something. It was a good experience for me. I learned how giving something up can make you really focus on it. I also learned never to give up something you cannot live without. Like yummy, delicious dessert!

Grace enjoys writing short stories, especially when visiting Vermont. After school, she plays basketball, softball, and tennis and competes on a swim team.

Charlotte took the DARE

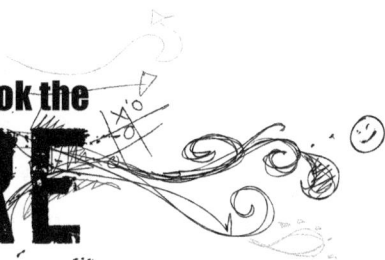

I Want to Go Home
By Charlotte Boin, Grade 6

I'm not naturally a daring person. I can be described as nice. Generous. Friendly. A bit quick-tempered, maybe. But cautious.

As I was hunting through the Internet, though, looking for a suitable writing contest, "Take the Dare: Dare to be You!" caught my eye. So here I am.

At first I had no idea what to write about. My sister? No. But what else?

The topic I picked is probably not seen very often. It's just a personal thing I have. I catch myself doing it way too much.

Before I start, I'll have to explain something. I'm multi-cultured—half Dutch, half American—and

I've lived in Holland for nearly all my life, except a year in North Carolina and nearly three years here in Louisiana. I think of Holland as my home.

I miss my home.

But—and here's what I'm going to write about—I think I say that out loud just a bit too much. At school, I say now and then (once or twice a week), "I want to go home," or "I miss my home." Nobody realizes I'm talking about Holland. They think I just want to go home. A half-hour drive away from my school, on Highland. They never think beyond that.

At home, when I tell my mother I miss Holland, she says, "Well, don't! You're going back soon anyway." End of discussion.

If I asked my friends, any of them, "How often have you heard me say something like, 'I want to go home?'" they'd realize I say it often. And I bet they've never thought about it before.

I apologize if I'm complaining too much (and I am), but it nearly hurts—thinking how nobody but my friend Coleen realizes what I really meant. Because she did, once. I can't tell you how happy that made me feel.

Saying "I want to go home," or anything of the sort, helps me. It pours out some of the misery I'm holding in. Now I'm thinking that maybe I should be glad not many people have realized what I truly mean. It might make them sad—and that's not at all what I want.

I'm not even sure *what* I want, what I'd gain by

saying "I want to go home." Relief? Understanding? Sympathy? Pity?

All I do know is that I want to stop saying those things. I don't want to be somebody who passes on misery to others.

So I tried this week. I can't tell you how hard it was. The relief of saying "I want to go home!" had been like a drug. My misery built up inside me, choking me, and I couldn't release it. I couldn't even whisper it in the dark to myself.

I wasn't happy. I'd never realized how saying those things helped me. But the thing is, I started writing this essay, and instantly I felt better. I'm pouring my feelings onto a blank page. Taking them out and stuffing them onto a blank page, which will store my thoughts without scolding me for them or feeling pain. And—just like that—I got why I love to write so much. You don't have to keep those things inside you because they will suffocate you in the end if you keep them there. The stress just keeps building up. Now I get what people are saying when they use the expression "blowing off steam." I never understood it before. Negative feelings *are* like steam, and you'll explode if you don't get them out of your body quick.

Talking to family—sometimes, it doesn't help. Sometimes they don't get it. Blank pages and pillows— my two main confidantes—will take in anything without arguing or pointing out I'm wrong. Because sometimes, you just don't want to hear it.

Now if you'll excuse me, I've got to run—my diary's calling and I haven't written in it in a while.

Dear Diary,

I want to go home.

Charlotte was born in the Netherlands. She's lived in North Carolina, Louisiana, and Holland. She loves reading and writing.

Kalen took the DARE

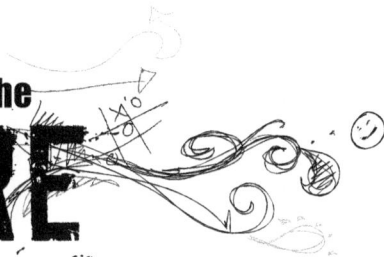

The First Step
By Kalen Gillingham, Grade 6

"But Mom! I didn't do anything!" I complained.

"So, you didn't kick your brother?" Mom asked.

"Well, I did, but he kicked me first!"

"He's only eight," Mom replied. "He doesn't know any better."

"You always use the same excuse," I said. "'He's only eight! He doesn't know any better.' So when Jack's twelve and I'm sixteen, you're going to say the same thing?"

"You always have to have the last word," Mom said.

My mom gets me so angry sometimes. She says that I always have to have the last word. Have you heard her argue with me? I think it's the other way around.

I'm Kalen and I have three siblings who make me want to tear my hair out. We all go to the same school and it's our first year there. At the new school, we have to make new friends, meet new people, and find our way around the school.

"Get out of the car, please," Mom said.

Wow, we're at school already? That was fast. "Bye, Mom," I said.

"Bye, Kay," she said. "Have a good day at school,"

"Like that's going to happen," I muttered under my breath.

I got out of the car and walked past the guys who always hang out by the student drop-off. None of my friends were here yet. I walked up and down the sidewalk, talking to no one.

One of the guys from that group came up to me and asked, "Is that your thing? Just kind of walking up and down the sidewalk?"

"There's nothing better to do and none of my friends are here yet," I replied.

He walked away.

I sighed. Where was everyone?

Alyssa finally showed up, then around the corner came Dana. Then came Emily and Katie, and then Taylor, and finally Clara. They chit-chatted away while I just stood there waiting to go inside. I laughed when it was appropriate, but I pretty much just stood there.

I wanted to be myself at school. I really did. But sometimes being you isn't who other people want you to be. And sometimes, you haven't been you for so long that it's too late to change. That night, before I drifted off to sleep, I hoped that tomorrow wouldn't be so bad.

I woke up to a bright, sunny day and decided that it was time for a change. I dared myself to be who I really am around my friends at school. And maybe I wouldn't fight with my brother and sisters either.

I got to school and I talked with my friends. At recess, I joined in on the basketball game and cheered on my teammates. And at lunch I talked about my exhausting night at dance. We played Truth or Dare and I wasn't afraid to do my friends' wacky dares.

Clara and I walked home after school together.

"You're a lot louder than I gave you credit for," Clara said.

"It was hard for me at first, but I got the hang of it," I said.

"The hang of what?"

I replied with two words, "Being myself."

Maybe life isn't so bad. My friends are a lot of fun to be around. As long as I keep it up, my life will truly become how it's supposed to be.

Kalen loves running and dancing. Three adjectives that best describe her are fun-loving, kind, and crazy.

Dami took the
DARE

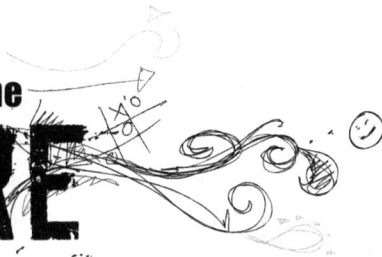

Turn Yourself Around So You Can See the Light

By Dami Lee, Grade 6

"It's my turn to be first player," I said.

"No, you're always first. It's not fair!" Sabrina exclaimed.

There we go again, off to another bad start. I wasn't really good friends with Sabrina, a girl at my daycare, but that was old news to us.

It's been about a week since I haven't said mean things to Sabrina. It all started on a stormy Tuesday afternoon, but that wasn't going to bring me down from being friendly. That day I didn't say anything to Sabrina, and I tried to sit by her and smile at her. The plan was a certainly not working because every time

I smiled, she would make an ugly face at me. I wasn't going to give up, though.

The very next day I started complimenting her, and I started trying to have a conversation with her as well. Although we ran into bumps, I kept myself from saying anything rude, even if she said something to me. Then I realized I was slowly becoming friends with Sabrina.

"Ha ha ha," Sabrina and I laughed. A few days have passed since I became good friends with Sabrina. We have said nothing nasty to each other, and the week has been full of joy. I am so happy to be buddies with Sabrina when I thought about all the good memories we now have.

I was so thrilled I could joyfully go to daycare, but the very next month I found out that Sabrina was moving to another state. I was so sad when she told me, but I was also glad I had made the right choice to be nice to her before she left. It was a rough road to drive on, but I had made it through successfully.

Dami found her passion for writing from her teacher who told her that writing is more than words on paper. It is a limitless expression of your creativity.

Ainsley took the DARE

Re:Strained
By Ainsley Doell, Grade 7

"Maybe you should just grow up a little!" I shouted.

Laughter rang in my ears.

I turned. My friend struggled to keep his composure, his shoulders shaking from the effort. I could tell he was itching to fling his head back and join in the laughter.

Was there anyone in this cruel world who would spare me some mercy? "You people think it's funny to go around making immature comments about my life?" I rolled my eyes. "How is that funny?" I demanded. "Maybe you should go get your own lives, and then you won't have to stand around commenting on mine."

"Come on, Ainsley," someone said beside me.

"You have to admit that was funny."

"No, it was most certainly not!" I said back.

It plays out the same way every time—daily arguments I have with certain individuals who constantly make fun of me. My tolerance is kind of like a balloon. It can only take so much helium before it pops and makes a very loud noise. After that last fight, I set a goal to get rid of my explosive tendencies. In other words, stop shouting at morons who deserve it. By reacting, I am only giving them what they want. Easy enough, right? Guess again.

The next day, the same people were at it again. I managed to make it through one ... two ... three immature comments. But then they said something truly offensive.

"*What is your problem*, exactly?" I started. "Because clearly there is something seriously wrong with you!"

I heard a small giggle from the commenter and I stopped myself. I realized what I was doing. *Okay, deep breath.... Relax. Good. That was a close one.*

Around that crowd, with immature insults flying left, right, and center, staying composed wasn't easy. I could only take so much. Eventually, though, day by day, I was able to last longer and longer without reacting to the remarks.

By the next week, when one of the bothersome bunch pushed his luck and made a comment, my reaction was simply, "Uh-huh. Sure." That turned out to be less satisfying to them than my shouting spouts, and the group slowly drifted away. I was able to stay much more mellow. Of course, occasionally, they would take something a little too far again, and I would get upset, but not to the same degree as before.

All it took to get them to give up (even if just temporarily) was to dismiss the comment as an example of immature behaviour or calmly pose a question like "Hmm ... and where are you going with this, exactly?" Or "I don't see how that would work, seeing as ... (fill in the blank)." Turns out, that frustrates them.

"It just *does!*" they'll shout.

Yup. Keep telling yourself that.

It takes more to push me over the edge now, but the problem hasn't completely vanished. Occasionally, I still get frustrated and yell at someone. A week is not long enough to develop a new, tougher skin, but I'm glad it was long enough to make a good start.

Ainsley is frequently accused of being a perfectionist and has a passion for writing short stories that she tears up immediately after finishing them.

Anthony took the

DARE

A Harmless Dare

By *Anthony Hope, Grade 7*

I took on a dare to be nicer to my brother because I am *not* a mean person; I am a kind person. I hoped to not only be more kind to my brother for a week, but also to become more caring to everyone I come across during my lifetime.

I chose this dare because I thought it would help me reflect on who I am. I am neither mean nor ignorant. I am gentle and caring. I don't want people to recognize me as "the boy who constantly fought with his younger brother." I would much rather be known as "the nice and caring young lad who always thought of others before himself." Sometimes I can be selfish, ignorant, rude, and bossy to other people, but I know

I can overcome that. My true identity reveals that I am *caring*, I am *kind*, I am *not* ignorant. All I have to do is let my true identity shine more than I have allowed it.

This is exactly what I did during my time participating in the dare.

I am not going to lie and say that treating my brother with more respect and being kind to him was easy. There were moments when I thought I couldn't stifle my annoyance with him. At first, the task seemed simple enough. Treat my brother as I would want to be treated for a week. I didn't realize at the time how hard it would be. My brother found out about me taking the dare, and he took it upon himself to be the worst he could be. He continuously infuriated me by singing aggravating tunes when I was trying to finish my homework, hitting and scratching me, and many more things while reminding me I *had* to be nice to him. With him doing this, it made my dare even harder to accomplish. In the end, I was surprised that I had accomplished my dare with only a few minor slip-ups.

Along with me messing up a couple of times during the dare, I did learn a few things. I learned that no matter how much my brother antagonizes me, I shouldn't let him get to me. He is younger than me and he looks up to me (as hard as it is to believe), so therefore I have to be the leader and set good examples. If I let him get to me, I honestly won't be any better than him. I feel so much better now that I have accomplished this dare. I was able to become kinder to my brother for not just a week, but in general. I have learned to ignore the small things he does to ensure I am not having a good time.

Once again, I am so glad that I have accomplished my dare. It wasn't easy, but I benefited a lot from it. I have realized that I have to allow myself to show who I truly am on a regular basis. I am not ignorant or mean, nor am I selfish or rude. I am *nice*, I am *kind*, and I am *caring*. Never again will I keep who I truly am bottled up inside.

Anthony is passionate about reading and writing. He also enjoys public speaking about global issues like child labor and human rights.

Mara took the DARE

Surprise!
By Mara Cobb, Grade 7

Most people think I'm not outgoing. They think I don't talk very much. Those people are really wrong! Since I have one little sister who talks nonstop and one sister who is usually babbling, I don't get to talk much. Even when I can get a word in, I usually still don't communicate. That's why I have dared myself to be more outgoing.

Sunday was the first day of my dare. There is a girl at my church that I hadn't talked to in a long time, so I emailed her. I asked her questions about school and what she was watching on TV. When she answered my questions, I think it helped me to learn more about her.

On Monday, I talked to my grandmother on the

phone. Whenever I write her letters, she always talks about how much she likes it when I write to her. So I decided to call her. She is 90 years old and cannot get out much. I think it made her that much happier when I called her.

On Tuesday, I wrote a letter to my great aunt, Ivy. It's a five-hour drive to visit her, so I have only seen her once, when I was nine months old. I make time to write to her as often as I can. When I write to her, it makes me feel like I can still keep in touch with her.

I did several different things on Wednesday. When we went to church that night, I talked to a boy my age about school and upcoming tests. In my youth group at church, I was the first one to volunteer to read to the class. After church, I talked to an elderly lady about recent earthquakes. She was so surprised! One of my best friends came with me to talk to the elderly lady too. The lady we talked to seemed glad that my friend and I stopped to ask her opinion about things.

On Thursday, my little sister had basketball practice. At one practice, my mom and I started playing foosball. A boy came along, and I started playing foosball with him. Later I found out that he was the coach's son, and he was eight. I kept on playing with him every Thursday for several weeks. Even though he was four years younger than me, we still had fun!

I called my other best friend on the phone on Friday. Even though I do not like talking on the phone, I talked to her for 45 minutes. She was going through a hard time, and I think I made her feel a little better!

Saturday was the last day of my dare. That day, my little sister had a basketball game. I saw a girl who had been on my basketball team the year before. Her little sister was playing against my little sister. It had been an entire year since I had seen her last. Even though I hadn't talked to her in a long time, I sat with her and talked to her through the rest of the game.

Throughout the week, I talked to four people I usually don't. I emailed a girl from my church. I talked to my grandmother on the phone. I wrote a letter to my great aunt. I cheered up my best friend. Not only did I surprise the people that I talked to, emailed, and wrote a letter to, I also surprised myself. I dared to take the dare, and I proved I am more outgoing than people think I am!

Mara loves to write. Besides gathering chicken eggs and playing with goats on the farm, she also enjoys playing piano and reading—a lot!

Alex took the DARE

A Hunger for Humility
By Alex Li, Grade 7

"Hey dude, listen to me." I tapped a friend on the shoulder and proceeded to demonstrate a sonata that I recently learned on the violin.

He raised his eyebrows. "That's crazy. How do you move your fingers that fast?"

"Why do you always show off, Alex?" someone later said to me. "We know you can play."

It was music class, and like usual, my class was fooling around the first five minutes with our instruments, waiting for the music teacher to come in and start the lesson. By this time of the year, it was clear to my peers that I practiced outside of school and could easily follow the curriculum.

It's really not easy to write about bragging habits without bragging, so please bear with me. Over the course of three years with my class, I have developed a reputation for being a "brainiac" whom you visit for a reference instead of Googling it yourself. It all started about three years ago when people started asking me for assistance with computers. When you're better than someone at a task, it can be painful to watch his or her clumsy execution.

I grabbed the mouse from a classmate and did what he was trying to do. He was thankful for the help and teasingly called me a show-off. That's when I started to feel the need to feed the reputation. This habit is not something I'm proud of.

Recently, I've been seeking an opportunity to challenge myself to stop being a bragger because it has no benefit to me and is potentially hurtful to others. Coincidentally, it just so happened that after training for a few months playing Scrabble with some classmates, I was planning on entering a Kids' Scrabble Championship.

The tournament was partnered play—my partner was Jackson, a boy with a reputation for excessive knowledge of English literature. We were determined to win.

My resolution officially started before a practice game, roughly a week prior to the tournament. When we won against our practice opponents, I blurted out politely worded, yet conceited, remarks. When this happened, I immediately regretted bragging because I was actually the learning beginner who relied on my partner's decisions. As I got better at Scrabble and controlling my arrogance, I replaced my outbursts with intimidating and irritating smiles. Finally, the unnatural smiles turned into plain silence and, with some reminders, evolved to handshakes and "good games." Days before the tournament, after mastering the ability not to rub things in while everyone else was mastering Scrabble, I was ready to not be a jerk.

On the big day, it was made clear that good sportsmanship was important. It was on that day that I realized it was the attempt at modesty that made me work harder to get noticed. In return, I put a lot more effort into this contest than I had previously planned.

Looking back, the day of the tournament didn't just mark one success. During one of the greatest hours of success of my life so far, I actually resisted bragging. In fact, it was the last thing I could've remembered to do. Winning the tournament wasn't even the best part. I realized that I had overcome one of my worst habits at the most tempting time. In my book, this triumph wins me another week of bragging rights. Or not!

Alex moved to Canada from China when he was only six. He has a passion for Scrabble, technology, and music.

Alexander took the DARE

Lazy Streak
By Alexander McCarthy, Grade 7

When I was thinking about what I would like to improve about myself, I instantly went to my couch to think. That's when it hit me: I should try and improve my laziness. Naturally, I was proud of my laziness, but I realized that being lazy had more cons then pros. Have you ever heard of the saying "Curiosity killed the cat"? Well, the cat wouldn't have died if he were too lazy to be curious. That is what I used to justify my laziness for a long time.

Still, I know there are many reasons why being lazy is a bad thing. I miss out on a lot of exciting things in life, laziness has a certain effect on my health, and I've developed a lot of bad habits because it.

Now let's see if I can actually accomplish my goal in a week. I think I'll start by napping.

So after two days of trying to achieve my goal, I realized one important fact—believe it or not, it is possible to survive a day without being on the couch for at least an hour. Usually I leave at least one hour aside every day for sitting on my couch and doing nothing. However, because of my improvement plan, I painstakingly cut down my couch time from one hour to ten minutes a day. With that new-found time, I went outside and visited more places.

It was hard and took a lot of adjustment, but I did it. After I accomplished this feat, I thought I was home free. I was wrong.

After conquering the couch, the next few days I tried to tackle my lazy bad habits. My plan failed miserably. I found that no matter how hard I tried, I could not overcome my lack of interest in doing manual labor. Usually, when asked to help move something, I spend most of the time thinking about how to avoid doing it. This often gets me into massive heaps of trouble. Even after five days of trying the plan, I would still find myself trying to avoid the work, then getting into trouble. So I learned that sometimes there are habits you just can't break.

Good things did come out of this, though. I broke my indoors habit and I am venturing outdoors more. I am no longer classified as a couch potato, although I still spend some time on the couch. Some things are hard to do, but I will not stop trying to curb my laziness. I know I will break this lazy streak, just not now. Maybe later?

Alexander lives in Scarborough. He occupies his time by going to school and talking to friends. He enjoys sports.

Ben took the
DARE

For Every Step You Take
By Ben Pinhorn, Grade 7

Comments like "Ben, you're so immature," "You are even more stupid than usual," and "You're officially an idiot" are said to me every day. The constant insults, although harmless on their own, have a big impact on my self-esteem and my opinions of others. They buzz around my head every day, and sticking up for myself never occurs to me. I just nod and laugh.

When I was in grade four, I was a very stubborn and extremely confident person. I had been a leader at my old school, so I held myself in high esteem. As time moved on and different people came into my life, my confidence slowly faded. I eventually got tired of it. I decided the only way to get my confidence back was to do confident things. That's why I decided my improvement idea would be to stick up for myself when I need to.

It is now a week later, and I am very happy with my results. I am planning on continuing my improvement idea until it becomes a natural part of my life. I have been mocked many times recently, and I have said something. I have either told the producer of the jest to back off or I've told them that I am through with it.

Most of the time, they have stepped back and looked at me with new understanding. People are saying fewer insults, and I am less hurt when they do say something. The gratification I am getting from this improvement is enormous.

Here is an incident where this improvement idea has backfired, though. Nothing is perfect, after all. One of my friends walked up to me the other day, and we started talking. He made a fairly major remark I'd rather not repeat, and I said, "Why is it always me you have to say things like that to? I'm not your verbal punching bag."

"Stop being such a spaz," he retorted. "Just chill. It was a joke."

As always, for every step you take, you have a chance of slipping. I refuse to just lie there after the fall, so I'm still not going to let people use me as "a verbal punching bag" even though I might have to get the hang of not seeming like a jerk.

The impact on my confidence is really starting to show and it has some positives in itself. People have always described me as a person whose moods are a little unpredictable. It hasn't stopped any friendships for very long, but I always try to be better. I am happier and more confident. I stay with one mood (and usually a good one) for a lot longer than before, and if my mood does change, there is usually a good reason.

My friends like me more, and I am having an easier time liking them. I don't get annoyed nearly as easily, and I have a lot more fun, too. An unusual side effect to writing this essay is that as people read and hear about it, they back off even more because they understand how strongly I feel.

In conclusion, I would like to suggest to anyone who is reading this that they take the dare if they are being picked on. It really helps. Try it. The impact is amazing and so are the after-effects.

Ben has many hobbies. He writes poetry, music, and stories, although the stories are for school projects. He loves pie but hates asparagus.

Jackson took the DARE

Spurred by Sugar

By Jackson Smylie, Grade 7

"BOR-ING!"

"LA-AME!"

Two of the most overused words within my negative repertoire. I blurt out these off-putting comments 24/7. Especially in math class.

My teacher felt my pain along with the rest of my classmates' while we did monotonous math work. He put on some music to serve as stimulating white noise. We gladly listened as we got back to our obligatory work. Then this awful song played—a heavy metal screaming match between rabid singers. I blocked my ears, shielded my brain from the monstrous sounds.

"Class, this music was for a purpose," our teacher

said, smirking.

At the dreaded word *purpose*, we all cringed.

"I want everyone to rate each song."

Oh. No big deal. Faces loosened and, surprisingly, no one's eyes rolled. He told us to be honest, and I was.

Next thing you know, I was getting spoken to about negativity.

After some self-scolding, did I stop the constant flood of gloom? No. Is it possible for me to tone down my pessimism? Yes.

Most certainly *yes*.

After the early-morning routine, someone made a remark about my downbeat comments. Brushing it off was simple; I didn't think anything of people's perceptions of me. However, the sole thought that crossed my mind upon hearing the numerous sighs was *I'm not a negative person!*

I never have been. Internally, there's always been a silver lining under my looming distress. But still, I knew I had yet to attempt to show the positive side of me to other people.

Then my teacher, a young, liberal man, proposed a dare. "By Wednesday, a week from today, if not one negative comment has entered my ears, I will give you a Mars bar. If I catch you demoting, insulting, or in any way putting down something in this room, *you* are giving me a king-sized, succulent, sticky caramel Mars bar."

The whole week was a struggle, I cannot deny that. I was tempted to quit, but my innate need to change dominated.

On the very first day, my own teacher put me to a test: incessantly playing Miley Cyrus songs (a singer I'm a HUGE fan of—not) and making me critique them. One by one, I had to improvise (but not lie!) and say something good about the song. When my teacher started playing "Hoedown Throwdown," I almost cracked.

"It's...interesting." I rolled my eyes.

One thing I've learned from this exercise is that humans will do *a lot* for sugar.

There were successes, failures, and teachers letting classmates off easy out of pity. To decide the fate of the Mars bar, we had to hire a fellow classmate as a mediator. In the end, we called it a draw.

Throughout the seven days, I changed from a whining, insouciant teenager to someone whose vibrant thoughts weren't always trapped inside a shell of negativity. Overall, I'd say it was beneficial—thinking about yourself from an outside perspective in an unbiased fashion. Whether it changes the course of my life, I don't know.

All I can do is hope.

Jackson has recently developed an interest in words and language. He enjoys tournament Scrabble, music, art, curling, climbing trees, and making videos.

Gabrielle took the DARE

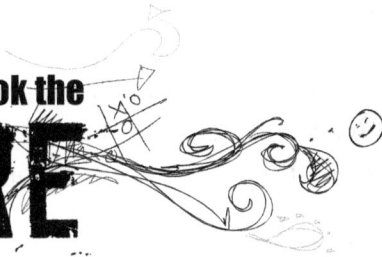

A Lesson in Truancy
By Gabrielle Tsilfidis, Grade 7

"Where is that kid?"

I recognize this voice; it belongs to my exasperated science teacher. I tell myself that I don't need the class I haven't attended in who-knows-how-long. I'm going to be a writer, or a filmmaker, or anything that doesn't involve science. This is wrong, and my subconscious knows it. Try as I might to eradicate the feeling, I like school. I like paying attention and learning, not dropping my books at the classroom door and running off to hide. Where's that goody-two-shoes who inhabited this same body in my primary years? I'm not a hopeless case though. Meta-Gabby still exists, under layers upon layers of carefully constructed film.

One week. I can peel back those layers for one week, can't I?

The first day goes more smoothly than I had any right to hope. Then again, it is the day where four of the six periods are classes I enjoy, and the other two take place in small, cramped classrooms with large, fierce teachers inside—the kind who never tolerate indifference in a child and care about kids' feelings. The type who still believe education is a privilege, not a right. And they might just be on to something.

Naturally, I hit a bump in the road. I can't go to French. By this point, it's clear that I simply can't force myself to be interested in nouns relating to any given topic, the cleverly disguised verb conjugation lessons that fit inside the tidy box of a French unit. Easily breaking my promise to myself, I hide my binder behind a garbage can and start to wander.

My mechanical meandering eventually leads me back to the door of the class I'm supposed to be in. Forcing myself to stand still, I flatten myself against the wall and listen to the result of my absence. It doesn't take them long to realize that my often-vacant seat is—surprise!—vacant again. *"Ou est Gabby?"* asks a classmate, trying to curry favor with the teacher while casting aspersions on my absence. He pronounces every consonant, making me wince.

"Come on, it's *Gabby*," someone says. "She's wandering somewhere, or destroying something." There's a smattering of half-hearted laughter.

Apparantly Gabby-never-shows-up-to-class jokes are getting old. I would have kept a perfect grade point average and cultivated my popularity (or lack thereof) if I had known six months ago that one day, Gabby Tsilfidis was going to be a *French room punchline*. I refuse to be an opportunity for some doughy, misshapen pre-teen to seem witty. Just as the teacher sighs, I open the door of the classroom. "I was just in the washroom, Madame," I say sincerely. And reading the graffiti on the walls was about ten times more interesting than your lecture. "I'm sorry I'm late." I'm also sorry for sounding like a fake, for being a fake, for being here at all.

The teacher composes her face in a fraction of a second. "It's okay, Gabby. Just grab a sheet. We're taking up the test on *les adjectifs*." It felt like at that moment, the intro bars of an upbeat song by some long-forgotten band should be playing. I should flash a twin-dimpled smile and a classmate should offer me a high five while the teacher smiles to herself, clicks her tongue, and thinks, *What will that girl do next?* My life isn't a lazily written Hollywood movie, though. I know that now.

Guided by my feet only, I walk to my next class in a fog. The image of all my teachers and me joining hands for a peaceful rendition of "Kumbaya" dances in my field of vision. The camera does a panoramic scan, and the newly exposed Meta-Gabby winks into the camera and laughs silently at some

hilarious joke.
    The credits roll....

Gabrielle is interested in music, film, books, and, when the occasion calls for it, writing essays.

Ryan took the DARE

Stop Arguing

By Ryan Vienneau, Grade 7

My sister walked in the room. "Ryan, can you turn on *Pajama Sam* for me?"

I turned to my brother. "Dylan, you go do it."

He said, "No, you do it," and we get into a big argument along the lines of this:

"You do it."

"No, you."

"Dylan, just do it."

"No."

"Fine, I'll do it."

As you can see, I have a problem with arguing with my brother over doing things. I am going to have to change. This is going to be tough, though.

Today was the first day that I wasn't going to argue, and my dare is already starting to get to me. My sister walked in and asked for me to put on her "show," as she calls it. I asked my brother if he could do it and he said, "No." I felt like arguing, but I said to myself, *You know what? I'm not going to do this right now.* I got up and put my sister's "show" on for her.

One of the things I'm noticing is that when somebody asks me to do something, I usually ask my brother to do it before I do it myself. This is something that I should change as well.

A few nights later, we watched a movie with my dad. My brother and I wanted to get some popcorn and a drink. We both wanted pop, but it was out in the garage. So I asked my brother if he could get it. He said, "It's too cold out, and I don't have socks on." I really wanted to get into an argument, but I realized that would ultimately end with me getting it anyway. So I just went out and got the pop. This saved me the trouble of having to get into a debate and we quickly got back to our movie.

Now, I'm not saying the dare was entirely successful. There was this one time that my sister wanted me to turn her computer on for her. But my brother and I both did not want to do it. So we got into an argument along the lines of this:

"You turn it on."

"No."

"Just do it."

"Not a chance."

You see where this is going?

"Come on."

"NO!"

"Fine, I'll do it."

By then, our sister had gotten bored and moved onto something else entirely.

So I've had a few small failures, but also some big victories. Just the other day, my mom called me to go put away some laundry. Instead of looking for my brother right away, I just got up and did it. I managed. I lived. It wasn't even so bad, and it made my mom pretty happy too.

I've learned a couple of things during this exercise. First, if I argue with my brother I'll still end up doing it anyway, and it might be faster if I just do it in the first place. Second, it does not hurt me to do things myself. Third, I do not really enjoy arguing with my brother anyway.

Ryan Vienneau is thirteen and lives in Toronto with his brother, sister, mother and father. His interests include sports, video games, humorous books and zombies.

Acknowledgments

First, I'd like to give major props to the essayists for writing some great essays and working in such a professional manner throughout the editing process.

In addition to the essayists, I'd like to thank the teachers and parents who championed the essay contest for their students and helped these young authors achieve, in many cases, their first publication credits!

I'd also like to thank Laura Kuhn, copyeditor extraordinaire. I can't find a typo to save my life and my English is good, but not that good. So thank you, Laura, for your hard work!

I'd also like to give a shout-out to Una Martin for putting together a great cover and designing the book's interior. It's hip and cool and everything I could ask for. Thank you!

www.ingramcontent.com/pod-product-compliance
Lightning Source LLC
Chambersburg PA
CBHW060532030426
42337CB00021B/4231